LOW VOICE

Disney
CONTEMPORARY
SONGS

10 SELECTIONS FOR SINGERS

D0907593

To access companion recorded
performances and accompaniments online, visit:
www.halleonard.com/mylibrary

Enter Code
6711-1775-7751-1668

Disney and Disney/Pixar characters and artwork © Disney Enterprises, Inc.

WALT DISNEY MUSIC COMPANY
WONDERLAND MUSIC COMPANY, INC.

978-1-4234-1279-3

DISTRIBUTED BY

7777 W. BLUEMOUND RD. P.O. BOX 13819 MILWAUKEE, WI 53213

In Australia Contact:
Hal Leonard Australia Pty. Ltd.
4 Lentara Court
Cheltenham, Victoria, 3192 Australia
Email: ausadmin@halleonard.com

Visit Hal Leonard Online at
www.halleonard.com

ON THE RECORDINGS . . .

Julian Brightman

Julian has sung from Broadway to the White House, and all points in between. Career highlights include *Peter Pan* and *Hello, Dolly!* on Broadway; *West Side Story* at the legendary La Scala Opera House in Milan; and *The Fantasticks* at Washington, D.C.'s historic Ford's Theatre.

Sarah Jane Everman

Sarah has appeared at the New York City Center with the Encores series. She has performed on Broadway in *Wicked, Wonderful Town,* and *The Apple Tree.*

Susan Derry

Susan has performed on Broadway in *Wonderful Town* (Eileen) and *The Phantom of the Opera* (Christine); and she has appeared as a guest soloist with the New York Pops at Carnegie Hall. She attended Northwestern University and received her Masters in Voice form the Manhattan School of Music.

Jeff Whiting

Jeff has originated numerous roles for Walt Disney Entertainment, including Quasimodo in Disneyworld's *Hunchback of Notre Dame,* and *Peter Pan* and *Young Hercules* aboard the Disney Magic, as a member of the original cast of the Disney Cruise Line's inaugural season. Jeff served as Assistant Director to the National Tours of *Hairspray* and *The Producers.*

MICHAEL DANSICKER, producer, has worked as arranger, composer, musical director and pianist on over 100 Broadway and Off-Broadway productions; from *Grease* (1975) to *Series of Dreams* (Tharp/Dylan Project '05.) His musical *Twenty Fingers, Twenty Toes* (Book, Music and Lyrics) has been performed Off-Broadway at the NY WPA Theatre and The York and his Boogie-Woogie Opera *Swing Shift* was performed at the Manhattan Theatre Club. He has composed original music for over a dozen plays in New York, including The *Glass Menagerie* (revival with Jessica Tandy) and *Total Abandon* (with Richard Dreyfus), and musically supervised the Royal Shakespeare Company transfers of *Piaf, Good,* and *Les Liasons Dangereuses.* He served as vocal consultant to the hit films *Elf* (New Line Cinema), *Analyze That!* (Warner Bros.), and *Meet the Parents* (Universal), and also scored the dance sequences for Paramount's comedy classic *Brain Donors* (starring John Turturro). In the world of concert dance, he has composed and scored pieces for Twyla Tharp, American Ballet Theatre, Geoffrey Holder, Mikhail Baryshnikov, and The Joffrey, as well as serving as pianist to Jerome Robbins and Agnes Demille. Michael currently works as creative consultant to Walt Disney Entertainment. For Hal Leonard Corporation, he composed the music for *The Audition Suite* (lyrics by Martin Charnin) and compiled the four books of The *16-Bar Theatre Audition* series. As a vocal coach, he works with the top talent in New York and Hollywood (including Sony's pop division). As audition pianist, he works regularly with important casting directors on both coasts, and for 15 years has played all major auditions for Jay Binder, the "dean" of Broadway casting. Mr. Dansicker's original music is licensed by BMI. He holds a MA from the Catholic University of America.

CONTENTS

Singers:
1 **Julian Brightman**   2 **Sarah Jane Everman**   3 **Susan Derry**   4 **Jeff Whiting**

Pianists:
*Ruben Piirainen   **Richard Walters

Vocal recordings produced by Michael Dansicker
Engineered by Chip Fabrizi at P.P.I. Recording, Inc., New York City

BEAUTY AND THE BEAST
from Walt Disney's *Beauty and the Beast*

Lyrics by Howard Ashman
Music by Alan Menken

Lyrically

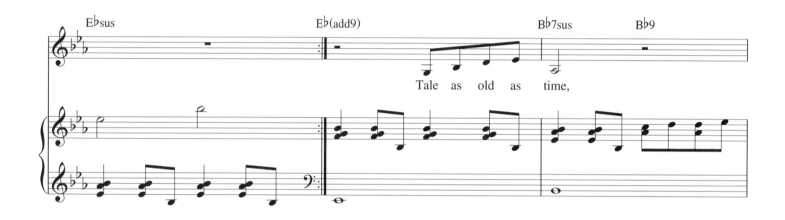

Tale as old as time, true as it can be. Bare-ly e-ven

friends, then some-bod-y bends un-ex-pect-ed-ly.

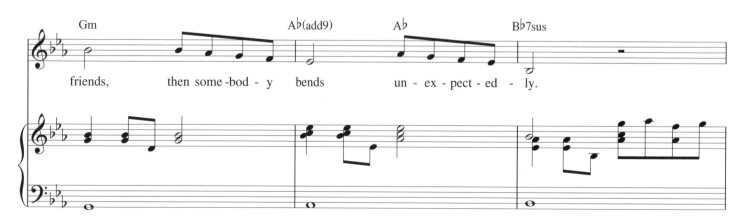

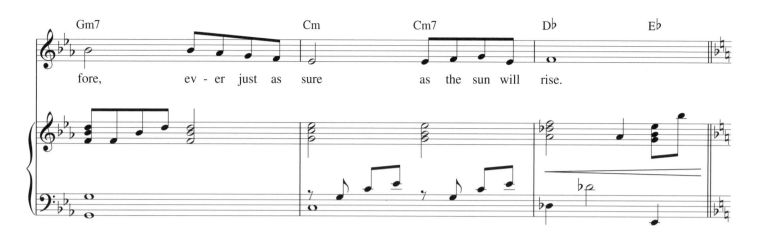

Gm7 ... Cm ... Cm7 ... Db ... Eb

fore, ev - er just as sure as the sun will rise.

F ... F(add2) ... F ... C7sus ... C7 ... F(add9) ... F

Tale as old as time. Tune as old as

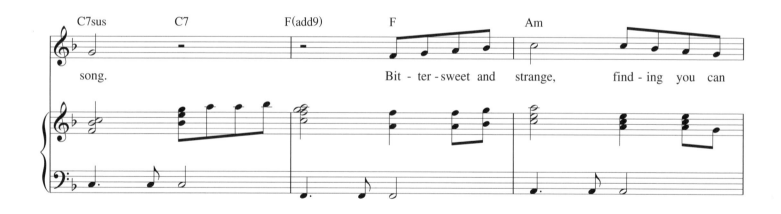

C7sus ... C7 ... F(add9) ... F ... Am

song. Bit - ter - sweet and strange, find - ing you can

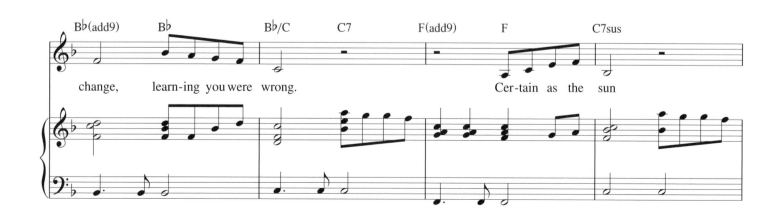

Bb(add9) ... Bb ... Bb/C ... C7 ... F(add9) ... F ... C7sus

change, learn - ing you were wrong. Cer - tain as the sun

CAN YOU FEEL THE LOVE TONIGHT

from Walt Disney Pictures' *The Lion King*

Music by Elton John
Lyrics by Tim Rice

COLORS OF THE WIND
from Walt Disney's *Pocahontas*

Music by Alan Menken
Lyrics by Stephen Schwartz

To Coda ⊕

F6 · C/E · Am7(add4) · Dm7 · F/G

paint with all __ the col-ors of the wind? Can you paint with all __ the col-ors of the

C · Am · G6 · F · F/G · C · G

wind? Come run the hid-den pine __ trails of the
rain-storm and the riv __ er are my

Am · Fadd9 · C · Em7

for - est, come taste the sun-sweet ber-ries of the earth, come
broth-ers; the her-on and the ot-ter are my friends; and

Am · G6 · F6 · C/E · Dm7 · C/G · G

roll in all __ the rich-es all a-round you, and for once nev-er won-der what they're
we are all __ con-nect-ed to each oth-er in a

GO THE DISTANCE

from Walt Disney Pictures' *Hercules*

Music by Alan Menken
Lyrics by David Zippel

This is the movie version of the song. The optional notes are to be sung if the lower notes are not possible.

GOD HELP THE OUTCASTS
from Walt Disney's *The Hunchback of Notre Dame*

Music by Alan Menken
Lyrics by Stephen Schwartz

24

PART OF YOUR WORLD
from Walt Disney's *The Little Mermaid*

Lyrics by Howard Ashman
Music by Alan Menken

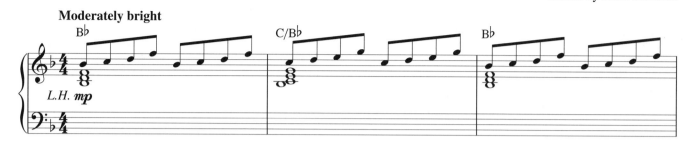

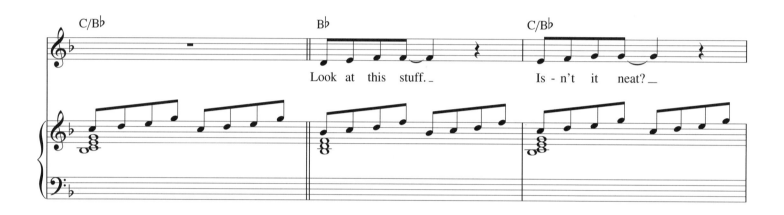

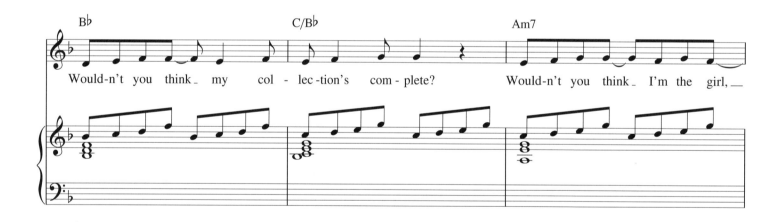

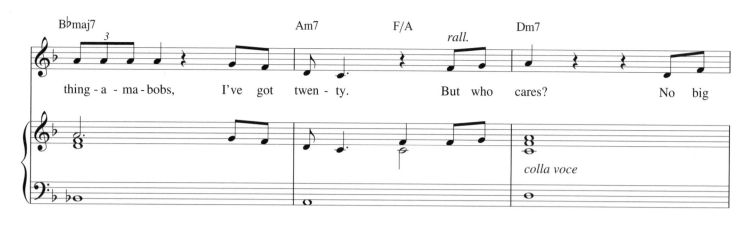

thing - a - ma - bobs, I've got twen - ty. But who cares? No big

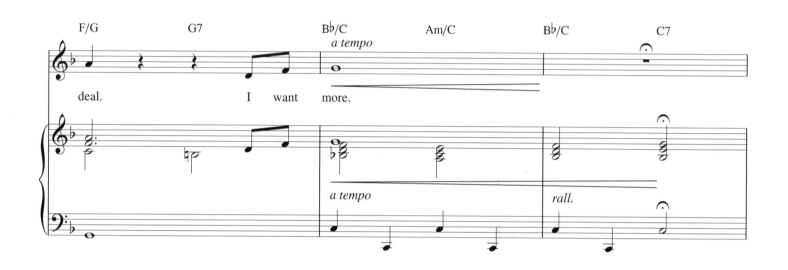

deal. I want more.

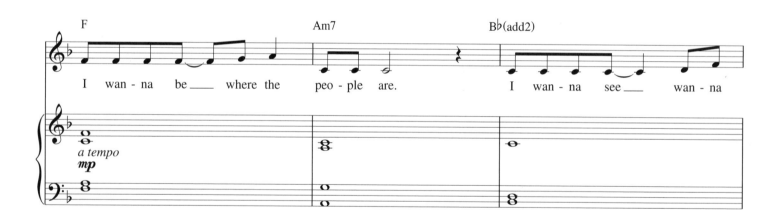

I wan - na be ___ where the peo - ple are. I wan - na see ___ wan - na

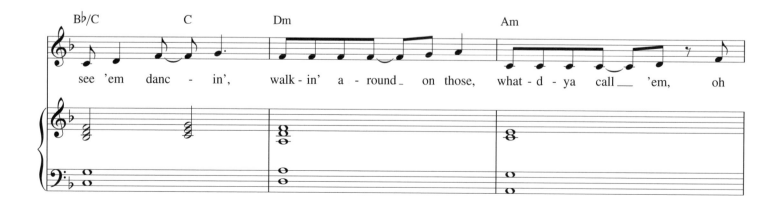

see 'em danc - in', walk - in' a - round ___ on those, what - d - ya call ___ 'em, oh

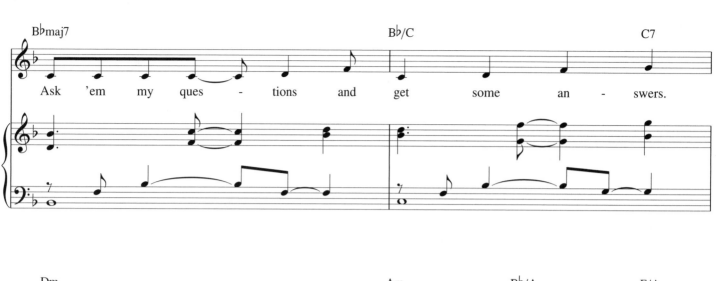

Ask 'em my ques - tions and get some an - swers.

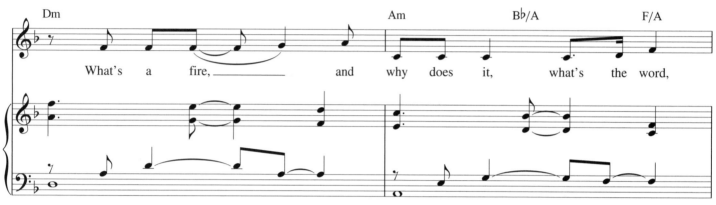

What's a fire, _____ and why does it, what's the word,

burn. When's it my turn? Would - n't I

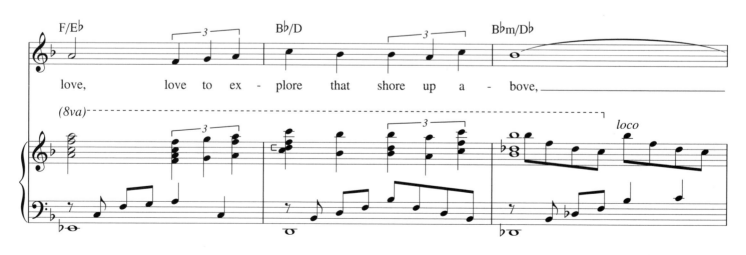

love, love to ex - plore that shore up a - bove, _____

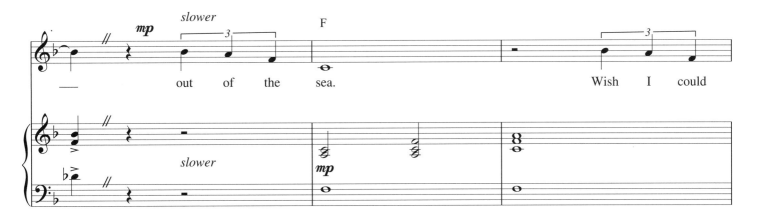

out of the sea.

Wish I could

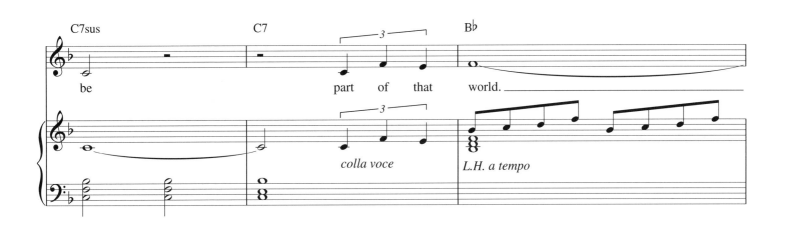

be

part of that world.

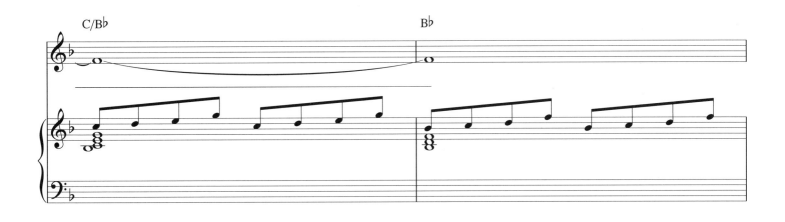

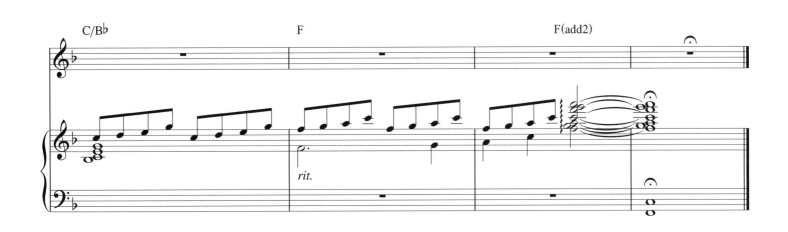

SOMEDAY

from Walt Disney's *The Hunchback of Notre Dame*

Music by Alan Menken
Lyrics by Stephen Schwartz

WHEN SHE LOVED ME
from Walt Disney Pictures' *Toy Story 2* - A Pixar Film

Music and Lyrics by
Randy Newman

When some - bod-y loved me, ev -'ry-thing was beau-ti-ful.

Ev -'ry hour we spent to-geth - er lives with-in my heart. And when she was sad,

I was there to dry her tears; and when she was hap - py, so ___ was I, when

YOU'VE GOT A FRIEND IN ME
from Walt Disney's *Toy Story*

Music and Lyrics by
Randy Newman

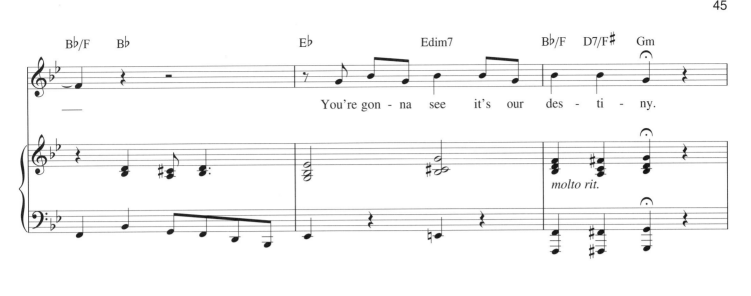

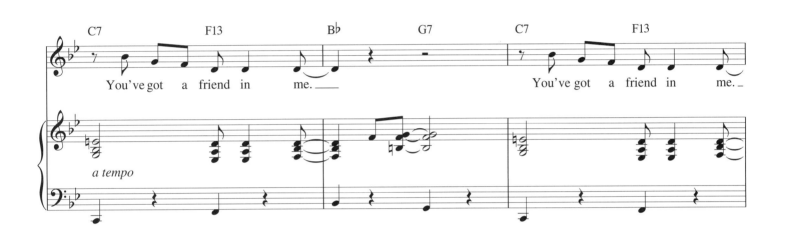

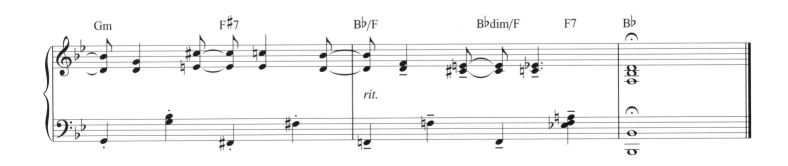

REFLECTION
from Walt Disney Pictures' *Mulan*

Music by Matthew Wilder
Lyrics by David Zippel

Bbm7 ... be my-self, ... Bbm7b5 ... I would break my fam - 'ly's ___ ... Ab ... heart. ___

Ab(add9) ... Who is that girl I ___ see ... Ab Fm7

Eb/Db ... star - ing straight ... Db ... back at ... Dbm(add9) ... me? ... Ab Eb/G Fm7 Fm/Eb Dbmaj7 ... Why is my re - flec - tion some - one

Gb ... I ... don't know? ___ ... Eb ... Some - how I ... Ab(add9)